Harriet TuBMaN

DK Life Stories

Harriet TuBMaN

by Kitson Jazynka

Illustrated by Charlotte Ager

Senior Editor Shannon Beatty
Designer Charlotte Jennings

Senior Editors Marie Greenwood, Roohi Sehgal
Editor Abhijit Dutta
Art Editor Mohd Zishan
Jacket Coordinator Issy Walsh
Jacket Designer Dheeraj Arora
DTP Designers Vijay Kandwal, Sachin Gupta
Project Picture Researcher Sakshi Saluja
Pre-Production Producer Sophie Chatellier
Senior Producer Ena Matagic
Managing Editors Laura Gilbert, Monica Saigal
Deputy Managing Art Editor Ivy Sengupta
Managing Art Editor Diane Peyton Jones
Delhi Team Head Malavika Talukder
Creative Director Helen Senior
Publishing Director Sarah Larter

Subject Consultant Rosemary Sadlier
Literacy Consultant Stephanie Laird

First American Edition, 2019
Published in the United States by DK Publishing
1450 Broadway, Suite 801, New York, NY 10018

Copyright © 2019 Dorling Kindersley Limited
DK, a Division of Penguin Random House LLC
19 20 21 22 23 10 9 8 7 6 5 4 3 2 1
001–314601–Oct/2019

A catalog record for this book is available from the Library of Congress.
ISBN: 978-1-4654-8542-7 (Paperback)
ISBN: 978-1-4654-8543-4 (Hardcover)

DK books are available at special discounts when purchased in bulk for sales promotions,
premiums, fund-raising, or educational use. For details, contact:
DK Publishing Special Markets, 1450 Broadway, Suite 801, New York, NY 10018
SpecialSales@dk.com

Printed and bound in China

A WORLD OF IDEAS:
SEE ALL THERE IS TO KNOW

www.dk.com

Dear Reader,

Can you imagine being hired out to work when you were six years old? Or having family members sold off and never, ever seeing them again? This is not a made-up story! Slavery in the United States was real. That's why reading and learning about it through the eyes of people like Harriet Tubman is so important. The past has many lessons to teach us, especially about how people treat each other.

Harriet was committed to freedom and helping others. From a young age, she stood up for herself and worked to change things for the better. She taught people to believe in themselves and their rights. I think she'd be glad to know that you're learning about her life. She'd be especially pleased if her story inspires you to use your voice for good, to care for others, and to work hard to achieve your goals no matter what challenges get in the way.

Kitson Jazynka

The life of... Harriet **Tubman**

1

A GIRL
NAMED ARAMINTA
Page 8

6

FREEDOM
Page 48

7

CANADA: LAND OF
THE FREE
Page 56

8

LIFE ON THE
UNDERGROUND
Page 66

9

GENERAL TUBMAN
Page 72

2

ENSLAVED
CHILDHOOD
Page 16

3

DEFIANCE
Page 24

5

FOLLOW THE
NORTH STAR
Page 40

4

TASTE OF
FREEDOM
Page 32

10

A NATION
DIVIDED
Page 80

11

LATER IN LIFE
Page 92

REMEMBERING
HARRIET TUBMAN
Page 102

12

VOTES
FOR
WOMEN

END
SLAVERY

Chapter 1

A girl NAMED Araminta

Harriet Tubman's parents named her "Araminta." This means "protection" in Old English, and she would live up to its promise.

Araminta Ross was born into slavery, a horrific practice in which a person is owned by someone else. But one night as a young woman, Araminta crept through the dark to escape. She was now a fugitive—a runaway. She would later tell stories of her experience, explaining how she slipped

through the dark, lifting her eyes toward the night sky. She searched the tops of the loblolly pine trees for a glimpse of the North Star—the star that would guide her to freedom.

As she walked along the river, she moved a little faster, ignoring the scratching branches, her sore feet, and the hunger in her gut. Freedom for the woman who would later change her name to Harriet Tubman, was more than 90 miles (145 km) away.

It was 1849 on Maryland's Eastern Shore. Many white people in the area, as in other parts of the country, owned people as slaves and forced their captives to work for them. These enslaved people, and their children, were the property of their owners, and could be mistreated or sold at any time. White people often felt entitled to use slave labor. How else, they would argue, could they operate their farms or shipyards?

SLAVERY IN THE UNITED STATES

The Trans-Atlantic Slave Trade started in the late 1400s, and over centuries, brought more than 12 million Africans, by force, to the Americas. The first enslaved Africans in what would become the United States arrived in Jamestown, Virginia, in 1619. There were about 20 individuals. By the 1860s, there were nearly 4 million enslaved people in the United States. The nation outlawed slavery in 1865.

Free states / territories   Slave states / territories

People in the United States disagreed about the slave trade. Some believed it was cruel, wrong, and inhumane. Some believed it was fair. Some didn't care. Others didn't like the slave trade, but felt powerless to change it.

As the young woman walked through the forest that night, she missed her family. However, Araminta (her family called her "Minty") knew that if she stayed, her owner would soon sell her. Leaving had been difficult, but necessary. If she made it to a free state like Pennsylvania or New Jersey, she could live free. If she'd stayed and been sold, especially to a state farther south, she might have been sentenced to an even harder enslaved life with little chance of escape.

She chose freedom—and she got there thanks to the Underground Railroad. This wasn't an actual railroad that transported enslaved people to freedom, although they did sometimes ride the train for part of

THE UNDERGROUND RAILROAD

Originally a loose network of abolitionists—people who believed slavery should be abolished, or ended—the Underground Railroad began as a small operation. It was started by abolitionists who offered guidance and care for enslaved people who had run away. Founded in the late 18th century, the network grew and became more organized. It provided an escape for enslaved Africans, and it also brought black people and white people together to work for good. In addition to the efforts of the Underground Railroad, black people had always resisted enslavement by not following orders or by running away to obtain freedom.

the journey north. The Underground Railroad was a system of safe routes and places. Hundreds of thousands of enslaved people found their way—through forests and along creeks and across fields at night—from one safe house to the next. Sometimes they "rode" the Underground Railroad all the way to Canada, but it wasn't easy. The journey required courage, quick thinking, and the ability to withstand hardship and uncertainty.

As a free woman in Philadelphia, Minty would change her name to Harriet. As Harriet, she would return to Maryland many times to help others escape. She risked being caught, beaten, or sold. But she wouldn't let danger keep her from helping others find their freedom.

DID YOU KNOW?

During wartime, Harriet led an armed raid in South Carolina, during which she helped rescue more than 700 enslaved people.

She became one of the most famous "conductors" (guides) of the Underground Railroad, leading many others, including family members, out of enslavement. She was famous for having never lost a "passenger."

But Harriet Tubman was more than a conductor of the Underground Railroad. Later, during wartime, she worked as a nurse, and even a spy. How did she accomplish so much, given that she was born into slavery and had no rights or money and couldn't read or write? All her life she fought for freedom and justice for herself and others. She inspired an entire generation of African Americans to fight for their right to freedom. It started with her smarts, her courage, and a deep determination to strive for what is right.

Harriet helped many people during her lifetime.

Gen. Harriet Tubm

Chapter 2

Enslaved childhood

Minty was born around 1822 in a run-down cabin on a small farm. She was the fifth of Rit and Ben Ross's nine children.

Minty, her mother, and her siblings were all owned by a young man named Edward Brodess. Her father was owned by Anthony Thompson, the owner of the farm where they lived on Maryland's Eastern Shore.

The area is part of a teardrop-shaped peninsula (piece of land jutting into the water) cradled by the Chesapeake Bay to the west and the Atlantic Ocean to the east.

Maryland

Atlantic Ocean

Chesapeake Bay

Creeks and wetlands crisscross the area's forests and fields. Ducks and geese splash in soggy wetlands, surrounded by flowering seagrass and plump cattails waving in the breeze. The area's fertile soil was good for farming.

Thompson was Brodess's stepfather. He took care of his stepson's property until he grew up. In 1824, young Brodess got married, and he and his new wife, Eliza, and all of the people he owned as slaves, moved to his farm about 17 miles (27 km) away. Sadly, even though his whole family moved, Ben had to stay behind with his owner.

The family was devastated, but soon they'd have to endure worse than leaving Ben behind. Brodess's bills had piled up, and in 1825 he sold Minty's teenaged sister, Mariah Ritty, to make money. At the time, Minty was a toddler. No one in the family ever saw Mariah Ritty again.

By the time Minty was five, she spent her days working, despite her age. She cared for her younger siblings, and perhaps a cousin or two until her mother came home. Rit worked in the main house and was often called on to labor late into the day.

Minty was good at taking care of little ones. For example, on one day around 1827, the sun had set after a long summer day. Minty's baby brother fussed—he was tired and hungry. Even though young Minty was tired and hungry, too, she grabbed his feet and gently swung him around until he giggled. She then cooked

a piece of pork for his dinner
in the coals of a dwindling fire.
After her mother got home, the
enslaved girl fell asleep in her mother's
bed—a wooden box filled with straw.

Minty had a loving family, but her
childhood was far from happy or safe.
When she was six years old, Brodess hired her
out to work for a poor farmer. The man arrived
to collect her on horseback.

There was no comfort in her new home,
and Minty's new boss provided little food for
her. The girl was made to sleep in front of the
fireplace in the kitchen at night. Hungry and
missing her family, she cried herself to sleep
at night.

The farmer's wife,
Mrs. Cook, planned
to train Minty to weave
fabric. But even at a young
age, Minty seemed to know that
slavery was wrong, and she refused to weave.
Instead, Mrs. Cook made Minty do outdoor

chores, even in the wintertime. Minty's job was to wade into the frozen swamp to pull muskrats from traps, and she worked without shoes. After Minty became seriously ill, Mrs. Cook returned her to the Brodess farm. The girl was of little use if she couldn't work.

Now about eight years old, Minty recovered under her mother's care. It wasn't long before Brodess noticed she was feeling better and he wanted to put her back to work. After all, the money she earned helped him pay his bills.

Minty had useful skills, such as caring for infants. Soon she had a new job looking after the baby of her new mistress, Miss Susan. Minty might have earned as much as $120 per year for Brodess, a large sum at the time.

What are Muskrats?

Short-legged rodents, about the size of two rats, that live in marshes, swamps, and wetlands of North America.

REVOLTS

When Minty was a child, there were many revolts, or rebellions, by enslaved people. There were about 2 million people who were slaves in the United States in 1830, and white people tightened restrictions in order to protect their "property." African Americans were no longer allowed to gather without supervision of a white person. In some states, black people couldn't own drums or musical instruments. In Louisiana, anyone caught teaching a black person to read could be sentenced to a year in jail.

Unfortunately, Miss Susan was cruel, and she kept a whip by her pillow in case Minty stopped rocking the cradle or if she let the baby cry.

Once Minty stood eye to eye with a bowl of sugar cubes on the table while her mistress argued with her husband. Minty had never tasted sugar, but had heard about its sweet taste. She reached out to take a cube.

Miss Susan saw Minty's hand reaching and grabbed her whip, but the girl ran out the kitchen door and down the lane. She jumped into a large pigpen and hid for four days. She ate scraps of food left for the piglets. When she finally returned, Miss Susan's husband beat her with a knotted rope. The punishment broke her ribs. Once again, she returned home to her mother in terrible condition.

"... I had **never** tasted anything good ... so I put my fingers in the **bowl** to take **one** lump and ... she **turned** and **SAW** me."

Harriet Tubman, quoted in *The Road to Freedom*, 2005

Defiance

Minty was smart and stubborn as a child. She saw the injustices of slavery firsthand, and it just didn't make sense to her.

Young Minty often wondered why African Americans should be forced to work when white people lived free. As she got older, she thought more and more about freedom—it seemed like an impossible, faraway thing.

When she was a teenager, Brodess again sent Minty to work at a neighboring farm. She later described the man who owned it as "close to the worst man in the neighborhood."

On a hot summer day she harvested flax. Blue flowers had burst from yellowing plants that stood about three feet (about a meter) high.

Blue flax flower

Her job was to pull the stalks from the ground, set them to dry, and brush out the seeds. The fibers inside the stalks would be used to make rope or woven into coarse fabric for clothing.

Minty pulled up plant after plant. The sweat poured down her face as she worked. Enslaved people doing this kind of labor were allowed few breaks, and they might only be given fatty scraps of meat to eat.

One afternoon while Minty worked, the cook asked her to go to the village store. Minty wrapped a shawl over her hair and went along.

On the way to the store, Minty walked ahead to try to warn another slave, a boy who was a friend of hers, that his overseer was looking for him. The angry man wanted to punish the boy.

what is an overseer?

A manager who is responsible for enslaved people's work and crop production on a large farm.

To try to stop him, the man threw a heavy counter weight—used to balance scales in stores—at the boy. Minty tried to block the overseer's way, but the weight hit her on the head. Her shawl may have softened the blow.

Counter weight

Minty returned to the farm, bleeding and dizzy. She lay on the seat of the weaving loom to rest, since she didn't have a bed.

Within a day or two, she went back to work, "with the blood and sweat rolling down my face till I couldn't see," she later said.

The incident happened around 1837. The injury left her with a scar, and for the rest of her life she experienced seizures, hallucinations, and vivid dreams.

what are hallucinations? Dreamlike states in which someone sees or hears things that are not really there.

Harriet believed her dreams and visions foretold, or predicted, the future. In her visions, she was herself flying free over fields and rivers, and looking down on them "like a bird."

She also had visions of frightened women and children, about to be sold. Minty, now 15 years old, was right to worry. Another one of her older sisters had been sold, never to be seen again. The Brodess farm was not doing well, but their owner could always make money by selling his slaves.

Around this time, her father, Ben, was "manumitted," or freed from slavery. Thompson

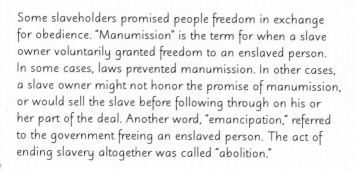

MANUMISSION

Some slaveholders promised people freedom in exchange for obedience. "Manumission" is the term for when a slave owner voluntarily granted freedom to an enslaved person. In some cases, laws prevented manumission. In other cases, a slave owner might not honor the promise of manumission, or would sell the slave before following through on his or her part of the deal. Another word, "emancipation," referred to the government freeing an enslaved person. The act of ending slavery altogether was called "abolition."

had agreed to free Ben when he turned 45. Rit and the children had the same type of arrangement with Brodess, but those promises of manumission were easy for an owner to overlook. Would Brodess sell off the people he kept as slaves before they reached the age of their freedom?

Now a free man who worked for pay, Ben convinced his employer, a man named John Stewart, to hire Minty from Brodess. Stewart owned a farm and a shipyard.

At first Minty worked in the house, cleaning, making beds, and walking Stewart's children to school, but she preferred to work outside. She was as strong and fit and as capable as any man when it came to outdoor work, so Stewart agreed.

As a field hand, Minty plowed, planted, and drove teams of oxen. She carried heavy farm equipment, and some days, she and her father cut down trees together. They sawed back and forth, one of them on each

end of a crosscut saw. They chopped off tree limbs with small axes. Then they would pull the timber down to the canal using mules, and finally load the logs onto ships at the wharf.

The busy wharf was filled with people. Minty worked alongside free black people, many of whom were sailors. They talked of places they'd been, and told stories about free states about 90 miles (145 km) north. Some talked about how an enslaved person might escape to freedom, traveling at night and navigating by the stars.

what is a wharf? A structure built along a body of water that enables boats to load or unload passengers and cargo.

UNKNOWN BIRTHDAYS

Most enslaved people did not know their birthdays. This was because slaveholders considered them to be property and, as such, they did not keep birth records for them. However, historians believe Minty was born in 1822. This is thanks to a note in a ledger—a book where people write down expenses—at the Brodess farm. It listed a payment for a midwife, who likely helped at Minty's birth.

Every day Minty witnessed the cruelty and injustice of slavery. She worried about being put on the auction block, where people were sold as property to the highest bidder. More and more, she thought about freedom—perhaps it wasn't so impossible or as far away as she had imagined.

"I grew up like a **neglected** weed— ignorant of **liberty,** having **no experience** of it. Then I was **not happy** or contented."

Harriet Tubman, to Benjamin Drew, 1855

Taste of **freedom**

By 1844, Minty was about 22 years old. Working outdoors had made her muscles strong, and she'd made a lot of friends at the wharf.

In addition to making her physically stronger, life as an enslaved person had taught Minty other useful skills. For example, she could stay awake all night despite being tired, and she could navigate her way through the forest and the marsh. She couldn't have known that all her life she'd been preparing herself to face the future.

She met and married a free man named John Tubman. Now her name was Minty (Araminta) Ross Tubman, and even though she was married to a free man, Minty was still an enslaved person. Any children she had would, by law, be owned by her owner, Edward Brodess.

Minty was smart. She had no formal education, but she learned everything she could about life outside of Maryland from the free black people in her community, such as Jacob Jackson, who was a family friend.

Intrigued by the idea of working for her own pay, Minty negotiated a deal with her owner. She agreed that she would pay him an annual, or yearly, fee of $60 so that she could work for herself.

JACOB JACKSON

Jacob Jackson was a free black man, and a friend of Minty's. It was illegal to teach enslaved people to read and write. However, as a free man, Jacob had both of these skills. Because of this, he was able to pass on messages between Minty and others.

She worked for hire, deciding who she wanted to work for, where, and when. Any additional money she earned beyond the $60 she paid Brodess was hers to keep.

She liked the feeling of freedom, and she worked hard. She made enough money to buy two steers (young oxen) to work alongside her. Now she could charge more for her plowing and farmwork because she had her own sturdy animals to plow with. She saved her money, but she still didn't have enough to buy her freedom from Brodess—to him, she was valuable property.

Unfortunately, Brodess's money problems had gotten worse. By now he had sold off three of Minty's sisters to distant southern plantations, forcing them to leave their small children behind. She and the rest of her family lived in constant fear of being sold. Would they be separated forever, too?

PLANTATIONS

Plantations were huge farms in the southern United States that grew crops such as cotton, tobacco, and sugar cane. Plantations could only exist through the forced labor of enslaved people. How they were treated was said to get worse the farther south the enslaved people lived.

Luckily for Minty, a serious illness during the winter of 1848 to 1849 might have saved her from being sold on the auction block. She couldn't work, so Brodess tried to sell her. But no one would buy her, because she was so sick.

SLAVE AUCTION

At a slave auction, or sale, enslaved men, women, and children were tied or chained in bare feet. Interested buyers poked, prodded, and evaluated the slaves' bodies. They noted their age, sex, and physical condition for work—human beings were sold to the highest bidder.

After Minty recovered that spring, she heard a rumor that she and her brother would be sold to owners in the Deep South to work in cotton fields. Minty prayed that it wouldn't happen because working conditions in the Deep South were known to be much worse. Less than a week later, though, Brodess was dead. "He died just as he lived," Minty later said, "a bad, wicked man." She wondered if her prayers had caused his death. It was March 1849, and Minty's husband believed that with her master dead, she'd be safe. He was wrong.

Edward Brodess's widow, Eliza Brodess, had small children and a lot of debt. By June, she had already tried to sell off Minty's niece Keziah (called Kizzy) and Kizzy's two-year-old daughter. Some enslaved people were sold to local farms where they could keep in touch with family nearby. Others, like Minty's sisters, were sold to slaveholders farther south.

Minty's anger and determination grew fiercer than ever. Her mother, now more than 60 years old, was supposed to have been freed at age 45. This was according to the wishes of Rit's original owner (a man named Atthow Pattison). Minty hired a lawyer for $5 to investigate the original agreement. The lawyer confirmed that Rit should have been freed.

Minty was furious. Had Brodess freed her mother when he should have, Rit could have stopped the sale of her daughters. Her original owner's wishes also specified that none of the family be sold outside of Maryland. The lawyer helped stop Eliza Brodess from selling Kizzy, Minty, and her siblings, but Minty would still have to fight for her own freedom. Her nightmares became more frequent—she dreamed about being chained at a slave auction. Minty called out in her sleep, "They're coming. I must go."

"EVERY time I saw a **white** man, I was **afraid** of being carried away."

Harriet Tubman, in an interview with Benjamin Drew, 1856

5

FOLLOW THE North Star

In the spring of 1849, legal complications had prevented Eliza Brodess from selling Kizzy. However, Minty was still worried.

It wouldn't be long before Mrs. Brodess found a way to sell her slaves. By September 1849, she went to court again for permission to sell Kizzy. Kizzy was the daughter of Linah, one of Minty's older sisters who had been sold years before and had never been heard from again.

Minty knew it was time to run, even if it meant leaving her family. She and her brothers Ben and Henry planned to leave that Saturday night.

Since Sunday was a day off, their absence wouldn't be noticed until Monday morning. By then, they'd be far away. Minty's husband refused to join them. Later, she'd tell her biographer, "I had reasoned this out in my mind; there was one of two things I had a right to, liberty or death; if I could not have one, I would have the other."

Working at the wharf, she'd heard about the Underground Railroad. She explained to her brothers how it wasn't a railroad at all, but a secret way north. The Underground Railroad had "stationmasters." Those were people—black and white—along the way who helped enslaved people trying to escape. Stationmasters provided directions, shelter, and perhaps a meal or a ride.

DID YOU KNOW?

Enslaved people on the run would often rub herbs on their feet to trick scent-sniffing dogs that were trying to find them.

Minty and her brothers set out on foot that night. The North Star would guide them, and she knew to look for the Big Dipper in order to find it.

A notice in the October 3 issue of a local newspaper called the *Cambridge Democrat* advertised a reward for "Minty, aged about 27 years, is of a chestnut color, fine looking and about 5 feet [1.5 m] high." The notice also mentioned her brothers.

"He (God) set the North Star in the heavens; He gave me the strength in my limbs; He meant I should be free."

Harriet Tubman, to Ednah Dow Cheney, 1859

43

MINTY'S GOODBYE SONG

When that old Chariot comes
I'm going to leave you,
I'm bound for the promised land.
Friends, I'm going to leave you.

A few weeks later, arguing about which way to go and afraid of being captured, the brothers decided to turn back. Minty didn't want to, but she returned home with them.

At home, the threat of the auction block still loomed. A few days after their return, she slipped away again—this time alone. That night, as she walked away at dusk, she sang a special goodbye song. She hoped those who heard her would pass the message along to her mother, her friends, and her other family members.

Her first destination was the home of a white woman who she had been told could help. Minty carried a quilt that she'd made from scraps and offered it as a gift.

In return, the woman told Minty how to get to the first "safe house" and handed her a message to give to the stationmaster.

Minty walked at night to stay hidden. During the day, she rested in hollowed-out trees or hid under leaves in the woods. When she reached the first safe house, a woman put a broom in her hand and told her to sweep the yard. This way, she could blend in, in case someone was watching. Anyone helping enslaved people on the run could be severely punished.

That evening, the woman's husband helped Minty get into a wagon. After dark, he drove her to the next stop or provided her directions on how to travel the rest of the way on foot. Minty knew that most of the creeks ran from north to south, so she walked against the currents—heading north.

SLAVECATCHERS

Slavecatchers were people who captured runaway slaves and returned them to their owners for money. They made as much as $10 for each person they caught and returned. Slavecatchers used hound dogs to search out runaways, and guns to frighten them into following their orders.

Minty's journey north to freedom was extremely dangerous. With every step she took, Minty was at risk of being seen and captured by a slavecatcher.

When she finally arrived in Philadelphia it was a relief—it was also a bit hard for her to believe. Was she really free? She later recalled looking at her hands to see if she was the same person after she'd crossed into the free state. "There was such a glory over everything; the sun came like gold through the trees, and over the fields, and I felt like I was in Heaven."

Freedom

When Minty reached Philadelphia in 1849, she became a free woman. Minty had by now adopted her new first name—Harriet.

In Philadelphia, free black people owned property and worked in a variety of jobs. The streets were filled with people—black and white—rushing to and from work and school. Vendors sold hot and buttery roasted oysters and fresh sweet corn to eat. For a few cents, one could buy a bowl of steaming Pepper Pot, a spicy West African meat stew. The area brimmed with free African Americans. Harriet soon found work as a servant and a cook.

Philadelphia around 1850

There was much to do in Philadelphia. Harriet enjoyed going to the public gardens and listened to intriguing debates and lectures about abolitionism and democracy. However, thoughts of her family back home in Maryland and their fate filled her mind.

She made friends with both black and white people who felt strongly about abolishing, or ending, slavery in all parts of the United States.

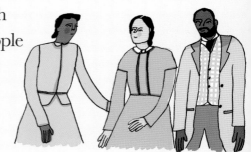

what is democracy?

A form of government in which citizens vote to help make decisions about how their country is run.

49

DID YOU KNOW?

When Harriet arrived in Philadelphia, the city was home to 20,000 African Americans, most of them free.

These people were also part of the Underground Railroad, which continued all the way to Canada. In Canada, slavery was not allowed.

Things were better for Harriet in Philadelphia, but they were not perfect. Kidnappers roved the city looking to grab African Americans and sell them in southern states. Many African Americans in the city were crowded into poor neighborhoods. As more people escaping slavery found their way into Pennsylvania, lawmakers from the southern states complained they were losing valuable property. They pushed to change the law so slave owners could retrieve their "property" from free states.

Harriet worked hard, cooking and cleaning and saving money. She wanted to free her family, and the money she saved would help her make the trip south again when the time was right.

FUGITIVE SLAVE ACT

In late 1850, United States President Millard Fillmore signed into law the Fugitive Slave Act. This law made it legal to capture and return enslaved people who had run away from their owners. This meant that even if they were living in a free state, runaways (called fugitives) were not safe from capture.

President Millard Fillmore

Unfortunately, within months of her arrival, a new law was passed, making things much more dangerous. The law was called the Fugitive Slave Act. Some people called it the "Bloodhound law." This was because a bloodhound was the type of dog often used to track down fugitive slaves.

Because of this new law, Harriet and her family—and others like them—would be in danger no matter where they went in the United States. Harriet decided to take action.

Harriet kept in touch with her family through a network of free black people who traveled between Philadelphia and Maryland's Eastern Shore. In December 1850, she received a worrisome message—Eliza Brodess was once again planning to sell her niece, Kizzy, along with Kizzy's two small children.

Harriet's dreams were again filled with terrifying visions of women screaming and hoofbeats of horses. She couldn't let her niece disappear like her older sister had. It would be dangerous for Harriet to return to Maryland, where she was a fugitive. She was brave, though, and she knew she had to go.

Harriet sent a message to Kizzy's husband saying she would travel to Baltimore, Maryland, and wait for him there.

Philadelphia

Baltimore

A rare photo of Harriet as a young woman (c.1860).

Historians debate what happened next, but legends say that an anonymous buyer (who was actually Kizzy's husband) bought Kizzy and her children, James Alfred and Araminta.

Almost all versions of the story say the auctioneers, or people leading the sale, were distracted by thoughts of lunch. While they went to eat, Kizzy and her children mysteriously disappeared. The story says that Kizzy's husband snuck them to a dock where he had a rowboat waiting. Then he rowed his family up Cambridge Creek into the Choptank River, then across the Chesapeake Bay—to meet Harriet in Baltimore.

Baltimore harbor around 1850

Harriet's abolitionist friends in Philadelphia likely helped them locate a safe house in Baltimore in order to avoid the city's slavecatchers. After they reached Baltimore, they would head to the free city of Philadelphia. There, Kizzy, like her aunt Harriet, changed her name. As soon as she reached Philadelphia and freedom, Kizzy would become known as Mary Anne.

Chapter 7

Canada: Land OF THE free

The trip to save Kizzy and her children would be the first of Harriet's many rescue missions to lead enslaved people north to freedom.

The Underground Railroad had helped Harriet escape to freedom herself, and she would use it for all of her missions. After the Fugitive Slave Act was passed, though, the Railroad was under attack. Slavecatchers searched the woods with guns and hunted runaways with bloodhounds—dogs known for their ability to track scents.

The Underground Railroad was made up of routes traveled on foot, or in rowboats or wagons, where the enslaved people could be hidden. Harriet and other "conductors" on the Railroad used secret codes to communicate without being detected.

THE UNDERGROUND RAILROAD CODES

Workers on the Underground Railroad used special code words to communicate with one another. Here are a few of them:

 Agent—someone who mapped out escape routes and made contacts

Canaan—Canada

 Conductor—person who took enslaved people from station to station

Drinking Gourd—stars in the night sky; also called the Big Dipper and the North Star

 Forwarding—the act of guiding "passengers" between stations

Passengers—people fleeing slavery on the Underground Railroad

 Safe house—a "station" on the Underground Railroad

Station—a safe place for "passengers" to stay

 Stationmaster—person who hid and helped "passengers"

They sent notes ahead to
"stationmasters," who were people
who used their homes as safe houses.
A safe house was a place where helpful
people provided food, shelter, and advice
about other safe houses.

A stationmaster might also provide disguises.
For example, a fake beard could change a slave's
appearance, and carrying a farm tool might
make an enslaved person look like a free person
walking to work. Harriet was known
to dress up in a silk dress, which a
runaway slave would never have
worn. Sometimes she dressed as
an old man and limped. Other
times, she carried a newspaper,
since people might assume she
could read and was therefore a
free woman.

After two successful rescue missions where
she safely guided runaway slaves from Maryland
to Philadelphia, Harriet became more confident.
She gained experience and knowledge of the

routes and the safe houses on each trip. Her support system also grew—and so did her determination to help more enslaved people find their way to freedom.

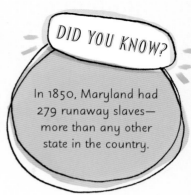

In the fall of 1851, Harriet embarked on what would become one of her most perilous missions. This time, she would try to persuade her husband, John Tubman, to come north. Returning to her hometown put Harriet in even more danger, since she could have been easily recognized. She sent a message to her husband asking him to meet up, but he refused. Harriet was shocked to discover he had a new wife—he had married a free woman.

Now she decided to use her trip to help others. She would guide a group of enslaved people,

including her brother, Henry, and his girlfriend, Catherine.

The day the group left, Henry left a man's suit at a secret hiding place near a creek on the farm where Catherine was enslaved. In secret, she changed into the clothes, leaving her dress in a creek. This way, it wouldn't be discovered right away. Disguised as a man, Catherine walked off the farm, and joined Harriet's group.

On their way north, it is said that the group of 11 people likely stopped at Frederick Douglass's home in Rochester, New York.

FREDERICK DOUGLASS

Born into slavery around 1818 in Maryland, Frederick Douglass learned to read, in secret, as a child. At 20, he escaped north, disguised as a sailor. He became an author and a leading abolitionist. He was a celebrity in his lifetime and spoke before large crowds.

A celebrated abolitionist, he was also a conductor at one of the last stops on the Underground Railroad before travelers reached Canada.

However, since the passage of the Fugitive Slave Act, Harriet no longer trusted the American government. So on this trip north, Harriet would leave Douglass's home and go beyond the border of the United States. She would lead the group all the way to Canada—where slavery was illegal.

Their destination was St. Catharines—a small town on the banks of Lake Ontario in Canada. St. Catharines is 16 miles (26 km) from Niagara Falls, New York. There, the Niagara River rushes north into Lake Ontario with Canada on the west and the United States on the east. A train bridge spans the river just below the misty, majestic, and massive horseshoe-shaped falls.

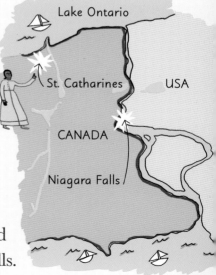

Lake Ontario

St. Catharines   USA

CANADA

Niagara Falls

Harriet took enslaved people across the bridge to freedom in Canada.

During the first half of the 1800s, trains crossing that bridge often carried fugitive slaves. Just like the river, they rushed north. In Canada, African Americans were free people, and St. Catharines in particular was known as a safe haven for those fleeing slavery in the United States. Former enslaved people had established a community there, and many American abolitionists spent time in the area.

Harriet was a leader and a well-respected member of the community in St. Catharines. She often spoke out about justice and African Americans' right to freedom.

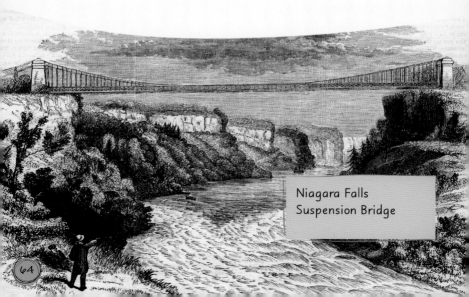

Niagara Falls
Suspension Bridge

Throughout the 1850s, Harriet would use St. Catharines in Canada as her base. From there, she would embark on her rescue missions south to the United States.

Harriet chose this area mainly because of Reverend Hiram Wilson, a resident of St. Catharines who was very supportive of Harriet's work and the Underground Railroad. An abolitionist, he assisted Harriet and her passengers upon their arrival, and a school that he founded was a "terminal," or one of the final stations, on the Underground Railroad.

8

Life on the **Underground**

Harriet stayed in St. Catharines during the warmer months, working to make money to fund her Underground Railroad missions.

When winter came, Harriet would head south to Maryland to escort enslaved people to freedom. By now, she had a great deal of experience and confidence traveling at night. However, for the people leaving home for the first time in their lives, the journey must have been both difficult and frightening. For them, it would have been no different from Harriet's first trip all alone. On their trips northward, the travelers may have heard wild

During this period, Harriet returned to the United States on many more rescue missions. She had help from close allies on the Underground Railroad, such as abolitionist Thomas Garrett, who sheltered runaway slaves and funded her missions. African American author and abolitionist, William Still, would later publish a book called *The Underground Railroad*, which describes the work of Harriet, and others. He also wrote of her new nickname—Moses. People called her Moses after the biblical figure who led his people, the Israelites, out of slavery.

9

General Tubman

Harriet helped many enslaved people get to freedom on the Underground Railroad. She repeatedly put herself at risk to help others.

After Harriet crossed the bridge into Canada with her parents in 1857, they reunited with their sons and their granddaughter Kizzy. Harriet's family members and other refugees who had settled there had become part of a thriving community of farmers, cooks, and builders. They started churches and sent their children to schools. Some owned land and could vote.

Harriet stayed in Canada for the summer, chopping wood and growing vegetables to earn money. But as usual, her mind was focused on helping enslaved people achieve freedom. With her parents safe and surrounded by family, she plotted her next trip back to Maryland.

By now, Harriet's reputation for bravery had become well known. She had convinced many enslaved African Americans to believe in their right to freedom, and other abolitionists sought her advice and help. Harriet believed in freedom and justice—and was courageous enough to risk her life for it.

In 1858, she met a well-known abolitionist named John Brown, a determined and passionate

John Brown

white man. Brown had led slave rebellions in Kansas and Virginia, and he believed violence was a necessary means to end slavery.

At their meeting in New York, Brown called Harriet "General Tubman," and asked her to join him in his mission.

Harriet believed Brown could help her cause and she encouraged other black people—free and enslaved—to hear him speak. She may not have supported his violent methods, but she agreed with his goal—to end slavery in the United States.

Harriet was a great speaker and storyteller herself. She gave speeches at gatherings in private homes, sharing Brown's abolitionist message. As the movement grew, she spoke at larger meetings and assemblies. Harriet shared stories of her own cruel treatment and how other enslaved people had suffered. Lastly, she called on everyone who would listen to oppose the Fugitive Slave Act.

On one speaking trip, she traveled to Auburn, New York. Through abolitionist friends, she

WILLIAM SEWARD

Born in 1801, William Seward was an abolitionist. He was a supporter of the Underground Railroad and a stationmaster. He served as a New York senator, then governor, and later, as an advisor to President Abraham Lincoln.

met New York senator William Seward, who was sympathetic to the plight of fugitive slaves. He understood that Harriet was also still considered a fugitive slave, and he admired her heroic work. He offered to sell her a piece of land at a low price, and she accepted.

Harriet liked the idea of being able to move her parents to New York because she

Harriet's house in Auburn, New York

wanted to have her family together in one location. Soon her parents would join her in the old house on South Street in Auburn, with its barn and fragrant apple orchard.

That fall, Brown called on Harriet to help him with a rebellion he was planning to carry out in the south. He and his fighters would raid, or attack, an arsenal in Harper's Ferry, West Virginia. He had hoped that the attack would give enslaved people in the area a chance to revolt and escape.

---

what is an arsenal? A place where someone stores and / or makes weapons and related equipment.

"I **bring** you one of the **best** and bravest **persons** on the continent— General Tubman."

John Brown,
1858

But Harriet was ill and couldn't come to the raid on Harper's Ferry. Instead of traveling south to West Virginia, she stayed in New York. The rebellion didn't go as planned and, because of this, Harriet's illness may have saved her life. Brown took 60 hostages (prisoners), but he was overtaken by troops and captured. He would later be hanged for his role in the failed raid.

After Brown's death, Harriet continued speaking in public to raise awareness of the abolitionist cause. She had heard news of large groups of enslaved people revolting and leaving the Eastern Shore of Maryland. Despite constant setbacks and hardship, she was confident that she would see the "jubilee" during her lifetime. That's what enslaved people called emancipation for all.

John Brown on his way to his execution after being found guilty.

Chapter 10

A nation divided

Harriet's last rescue mission was in 1860. In the same year, South Carolina was threatening to form a new nation—one that allowed slavery.

South Carolina was working to convince other states to join them in forming a new country. Meanwhile, on her final mission, Harriet guided people along the familiar route that ended with the bridge to freedom on the other side of the Niagara River.

History is unclear about how many missions Harriet made during her years on the Underground Railroad, or the number of people she rescued. The best historical estimates indicate she led about 70 people to freedom, but the number doesn't really matter. What is most important is that she inspired thousands to try to escape slavery themselves—that it was possible. She also helped people understand the importance of ending slavery.

In 1860, however, many white people felt their ability to enslave African Americans was their right. But that same year, Abraham Lincoln was elected president of the United States, and things were about to change.

ABRAHAM LINCOLN

The 16th president of the United States, Abraham Lincoln was born in Kentucky in 1809. He joined the military, studied law, and later entered politics. He became president in 1861, but was assassinated, or killed, in 1865.

President Lincoln, like Harriet, believed slavery was wrong, and his position on the matter outraged many people in the Southern states.

That December, South Carolina decided to secede, or break away, from the rest of the United States. By February, six more Southern states followed suit—Mississippi, Florida, Alabama, Georgia, Louisiana, and Texas. Together, they became the Confederate States of America. The rest of the country was known as the Union.

President Lincoln's first priority was to keep the country together. He wanted the Confederate States to rejoin the Union, even if it meant leaving slavery laws as they were. The Confederate Army wasn't satisfied with this compromise. On April 12, 1861, they attacked the Union Army at Fort Sumpter, South Carolina, which started the Civil War.

On July 25, 1861, Lincoln and Congress (the part of government that makes laws) declared war. In the North, the Union Army recruited available men to serve and fight, while in the South, the Confederate Army did the same.

THE CIVIL WAR

The Civil War lasted for four years, from April 1861 until December 1865. It was the deadliest war on American soil. More than 500,000 people died and another 400,000 were wounded. Many people think the Civil War was just about slavery. But really it erupted because of tension building from disagreements about how the young nation should operate, especially about the rights of individual states and slavery. The end of the war brought the country back together and expanded freedom and equality for African American citizens.

Union Army flag

Confederate Army flag

Fort Sumpter, near Charleston, South Carolina—the site of the first shots fired during the Civil War.

Map from 1861 showing the geographical divide between the Confederate and Union States.

Minnesota

Oregon

Dakota Territory

Washington Territory

Nevada Territory

Nebraska Territory

Utah Territory

Colorado Territory

Kansas

California

Indian Territory

New Mexico Territory

Texas

MEXICO

However, the president's declaration of war was intended to bring the states back together, not to abolish slavery. But many believed that a Union victory would bring about an end to slavery. With this in mind, the abolitionists went to work to support the Union.

Harriet volunteered to serve with a troop of white soldiers, and soon they traveled south. At Fort Monroe in Virginia, on the other side of the Chesapeake Bay, where she'd grown up, she worked as a cook and a nurse. Now fugitive slaves were called "contraband" and they were put to work. Harriet helped care for the penniless African Americans, many of them families with small children.

In the spring of 1862, Harriet and her troop traveled to Port Royal, South Carolina. There, she continued her work as a nurse. She used herbal medicines to soothe patients suffering from illnesses such as typhoid, malaria, and yellow fever. People called her a healer.

EMANCIPATION PROCLAMATION

Issued in the third year of the Civil War, President Abraham Lincoln's Emancipation Proclamation, or official announcement, allowed black men to become Union soldiers. Instead of being forced to fight for the South, they could fight for freedom.

The war raged on, but the Confederate Army had an unfair advantage—the support of enslaved people. In 1862, Lincoln signed the Emancipation Proclamation, a law that would free slaves in the Confederate States. It went into effect on January 1, 1863, and on that day, all the slaves in the South were freed. People in the North celebrated, but the slaves in the Confederate States remained captive.

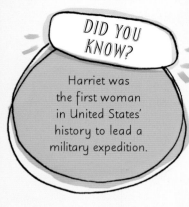

In fact, most of them didn't even know about the Emancipation Proclamation for months.

The war continued, but now Harriet could formally join the military. She enlisted in the Union Army and worked as a spy. She created escape routes for slaves in the South, whose owners refused to free them.

In 1863, Harriet made history in one of the most important raids of the Civil War—the Combahee River Raid. In it, she led a troop of 150 black soldiers in a surprise attack on slaveholders in South Carolina who were not abiding by the Emancipation Proclamation.

Before the raid, Harriet led a group of scouts on a dangerous expedition. In it, they scoped out the area and planned their attack.

Their plan worked. On the night of June 2, 1863, they launched their attack on the banks of the Combahee River. Harriet and her troops showed incredible skill and bravery. Despite being shot at by Confederate soldiers and local slaveholders, they managed to free more than 700 slaves.

But Harriet's military accomplishments did not end there. She would also work alongside a famous regiment comprised of African American soldiers—the 54th Massachusetts Volunteer Infantry Regiment. Harriet was with them at the battle of Fort

54TH MASSACHUSETTS REGIMENT

The bravery of the 54th Massachusetts Volunteer Infantry Regiment helped convince Northern leaders that African Americans should fight alongside white soldiers. For his courage in the battle of Fort Wagner, one soldier—Sergeant William Carney—became the first African American to earn a Medal of Honor, the country's highest military award.

The 1989 film *Glory* tells the story of the 54th Massachusetts Volunteer Infantry Regiment.

Wagner in South Carolina. The battle took place on July 18, 1863, and would later be dramatized in the award-winning film, *Glory*.

Harriet got sick in the spring of 1864 and returned to New York to recover. Then, in early 1865, she went back to war working as a nurse in Washington, D.C. It wasn't long before the Confederate Army surrendered, ending the Civil War. Lincoln signed the 13th Amendment to the Constitution, which abolished, or ended, slavery in the United States. Now 4 million African Americans were free, and the Jubilee that Harriet had dreamed of her entire life had finally occurred.

However, things were far from perfect. On a train heading north from Washington, D.C., a conductor refused to honor her military pass. Harriet was thrown into the baggage car and injured. Even though black people were now free by law, they were not treated as equals. There was still work to do.

Chapter 11

Later in life

After the war ended, Harriet continued on her mission. She would dedicate her efforts to helping former slaves and the elderly.

Harriet was now in her early forties. She had returned to Auburn, New York, where she would live for the rest of her life. Throughout the years, she had suffered from the effects of the injuries and illnesses she'd endured in her younger life. Still, she took care of everyone else, including her elderly parents. Many other family members had joined them in Auburn, and

Harriet enjoyed a community rich with family and friends.

Despite her fame and hard work, though, Harriet still struggled to make enough money to support herself.

Even so, she was very generous, and shared whatever she had. She always took in former slaves, whether they needed a meal or a place to stay.

Harriet had made significant contributions—both as nurse and soldier—during the war without being paid. She knew that she deserved payment for her work, though. So she applied for government compensation, or payment, but her application stalled for years. Even though slavery was now illegal, black Americans like Harriet still suffered a great deal of racism and unfair treatment.

RACISM—FREE, BUT NOT EQUAL

After the Civil War, the 13th Amendment emancipated all enslaved people in the United States. Although they were American citizens now, they still faced enormous challenges, such as hostility and violence from many white people about equal rights. In addition, African Americans were not given equal access to education and employment.

In 1869, she partnered with an admiring author, Sarah Bradford, to write her biography. It was called *Scenes in the Life of Harriet Tubman*, and sales of the book provided Harriet with some income. The same year, she met and married a Civil War veteran and brickmaker named Nelson Davis. He was very sick when they got married, and Harriet nursed him for many years.

In 1874, the couple adopted a baby girl named Gertie. She grew up in a warm and caring home, along with Harriet's mother and boarders, who were like members of the family.

What are boarders?

People who live and have meals in someone else's home in exchange for pay.

In 1880, their snug wooden farmhouse was destroyed by fire. Fortunately, Harriet, her family, and the boarders survived, and Harriet and Nelson soon rebuilt the house with sturdy brick.

DID YOU KNOW?

In 1899, Harriet was finally granted payment for her work in the Union Army—35 years after she applied!

Sadly, Nelson died eight years later. Harriet applied for a widow's pension, but her payments were slow to come. Finally, in 1890, she began to receive $8 per month from the United States government. She would have been 68 years old then, and it was the first time in her life that she didn't have to worry about money. Back then, $8 a month went a long way. She could live more comfortably now, but she still tended her garden to feed those around her.

Harriet (far left) with her adopted daughter, Gertie; her second husband, Nelson; and some of their friends and family, c.1880s.

QUEEN VICTORIA

In 1897, in honor of the 60th anniversary of her reign, the queen of Great Britain, Queen Victoria, rewarded distinguished individuals, including Harriet Tubman, with a silver medal. The queen also sent Harriet a lace shawl, which visitors can still see at the Smithsonian today.

While some might have sat back and enjoyed an easy life at this point, Harriet continued to work for equal rights. News of her work spanned the world—even the queen of Great Britain knew about Harriet.

Harriet was an especially strong supporter of the rights of African American women. She gave many speeches on behalf of women's suffrage and supported organizations that promoted the opinions of black women.

what is women's suffrage?

Women's right to vote. Women in the United States did not win the right to vote until 1920.

Harriet also wanted to protect the rights of the elderly. She had long dreamed of establishing a home for the elderly, and in 1896, she took action. Harriet got a loan to buy 25 acres (10 hectares) near her home. The property included a big farmhouse with a wide front porch, which was perfect for rocking chairs. In 1903, she donated the land to her local church. Then, in 1908, the church raised money in her honor and opened the Harriet Tubman Home for the Aged. On June 23, 1908, Harriet was the guest of honor at its opening celebration, surrounded by her family, including her grand-nieces and grand-nephews.

In 1911, Harriet underwent brain surgery. Sadly, ever since the head injury she'd suffered as a teenager, she'd had terrible headaches and a buzzing in her head. After the surgery, she moved into the facility that was named in her honor. At 91 years old, her strength had finally given way, and she was frail. Two years later, she passed away in the home she'd created, once again surrounded by loved ones. She was buried with military honors at Fort Hill Cemetery near her home in Auburn.

Harriet helped
others right up
until the end
of her own life.

Chapter 12

REMEMBERING **Harriet Tubman**

Today, many people know Harriet Tubman as a conductor on the Underground Railroad and a symbol of freedom.

That part of her story is true. But her heroism extended way beyond the Underground Railroad. She was also an abolitionist, a Civil War spy, and a suffragist who campaigned for the rights of women to vote.

Harriet devoted her life to caring for others and fighting for what she believed to be right. Tales of her daring and brave rescues also inspired many enslaved people to believe they deserved freedom. She inspired generations to stand up for justice, speak up, and take action.

END SLAVERY

VOTES FOR WOMEN

Harriet Tubman was well-respected and well-known during her lifetime, and her fame grew after her death. By the end of the 1900s, she had become one of the most famous pre-Civil War Americans ever known. Today, almost two centuries after her birth, people remain inspired by her story. Her legacy continues to encourage people to think about the importance of freedom, equality, liberation, and civil rights.

Monuments to Harriet have been built—from New York and Boston to Ghana in West Africa. There are buildings and schools named in her honor.

DID YOU KNOW?

Despite Harriet's hard work and her reputation, she suffered financial difficulties for most of her life.

The Harriet Tubman Monument in Boston

In 2013, on the 100th anniversary of her death, officials laid out plans for a 17-acre (7-hectare) Harriet Tubman Underground Railroad State Park on land near where she was once enslaved. Today it includes a visitor center and walking trail. The state also made plans for a 125-mile (200-km) driving tour, dubbed the Harriet Tubman Underground Railroad Byway, which winds through Maryland's Eastern Shore. There is also a Harriet Tubman National Historical Park in Auburn, New York, and a museum in her honor in Cambridge, Maryland. A 1978 TV

Cicely Tyson as Harriet

miniseries, *A Woman Called Moses*, starring Cicely Tyson as Harriet, celebrated her life.

In 2016, Harriet was also nominated to appear on the United States' $20 bill. The new design would be the first time a black woman would

Mural at the Harriet
Tubman Memorial
Garden in Maryland

appear on the front of United States' paper currency.

Visiting the Smithsonian National Museum of African American History and Culture in Washington, D.C., a person will find many of Harriet's personal belongings, from ordinary items like a knife and fork to a delicate silk and lace shawl, given to her by Britain's Queen Victoria in around 1897.

Shawl given to Harriet by Queen Victoria

Every year, Harriet's church in Auburn, New York, hosts a pilgrimage. Hundreds of people pray and sing at her gravesite at Fort Hill Cemetery on Fort Street to celebrate her life and her triumphs.

Those triumphs grew out of what must have been terrifying and painful situations. Harriet showed great courage, determination, and grit, even in the face of frustrations and setbacks. The fact that she never stopped working to help others find freedom and equality is a big part of her story. Grandchildren and great-grandchildren of the people she rescued can thank Harriet for their lives.

Harriet was beaten and subject to unfair laws. She walked thousands of miles during her lifetime, risking her life to lead enslaved people to freedom. Even though she couldn't read, her words and her actions made people think and feel. She inspired people to act.

Harriet was called many things in her life—Minty, Moses, a fugitive, General Tubman, and, later in life, Aunt Harriet. Perhaps the greatest thing she is known for is having never given up. She never stopped believing and fighting for what she believed in: freedom and justice.

109

Harriet's family tree

Linah Ross
c.1808–unknown

Sister

Mariah Ritty Ross
c.1811–unknown

Sister

Soph Ross
c.1813–unknown

Sister

Robert Ross
c.1816–unknown

Brother

First husband

John Tubman
1820–1867

Harriet Tubman
c.1822–1913

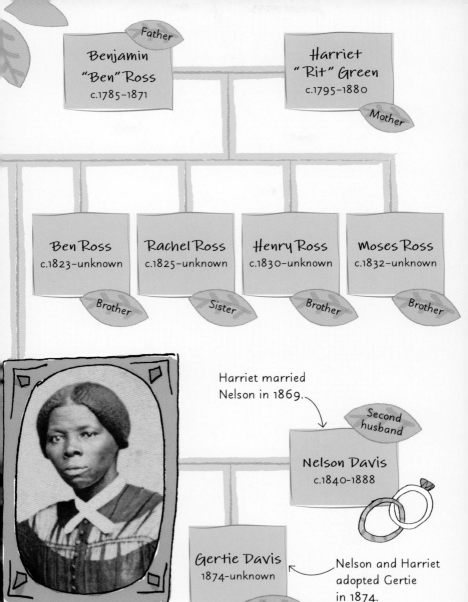

Benjamin "Ben" Ross
c.1785–1871

Father

Harriet "Rit" Green
c.1795–1880

Mother

Ben Ross
c.1823–unknown

Brother

Rachel Ross
c.1825–unknown

Sister

Henry Ross
c.1830–unknown

Brother

Moses Ross
c.1832–unknown

Brother

Harriet married Nelson in 1869.

Second husband

Nelson Davis
c.1840–1888

Gertie Davis
1874–unknown

Nelson and Harriet adopted Gertie in 1874.

Adopted daughter

Timeline

Harriet is hit on the head with a heavy weight, causing her to have seizures and hallucinations for the rest of her life.

Harriet runs away to Philadelphia, a free city, where she finds work as a servant and cook.

Araminta "Minty" Ross is born in Maryland.

Harriet marries John Tubman, a free black man.

1822   **1828**   **1837**   **1844**   **1849**

At six years old, Harriet is first hired out to work for a farmer.

Edward Brodess, Harriet's owner, dies. Harriet then hires a lawyer, to help stop Eliza Brodess (Brodess's widow) from selling Harriet and her family.

Harriet buys
a home from
William Seward in
Auburn, New York.

After two other successful
rescue missions, Harriet
returns to lead her brother and
nine other people to freedom.

Harriet leads her
niece Kizzy and
Kizzy's family
to freedom.

1850　　**1851**　　**1854**　　**1857**　　**1859**

Harriet leads her
brothers Ben and
Robert to freedom.

Harriet helps
her parents escape
to Canada.

Abolitionist John
Brown leads a
failed raid on
Harper's Ferry,
which results in
his death.

The Fugitive Slave
Act is signed into
law by President
Millard Fillmore.

Harriet makes her final Underground Railroad rescue mission.

President Lincoln signs the Emancipation Proclamation, which goes into effect on January 1, 1863.

Harriet formally enlists in the Union Army and works as a spy. She leads the Combahee River Raid, which frees more than 700 slaves.

1860   1861   1862   1863   1865   1867

The Civil War begins, and Harriet volunteers to serve as a cook and nurse with the Union Army.

The Civil War ends. Lincoln signs the 13th Amendment to the Constitution, which abolishes slavery.

John Tubman dies.

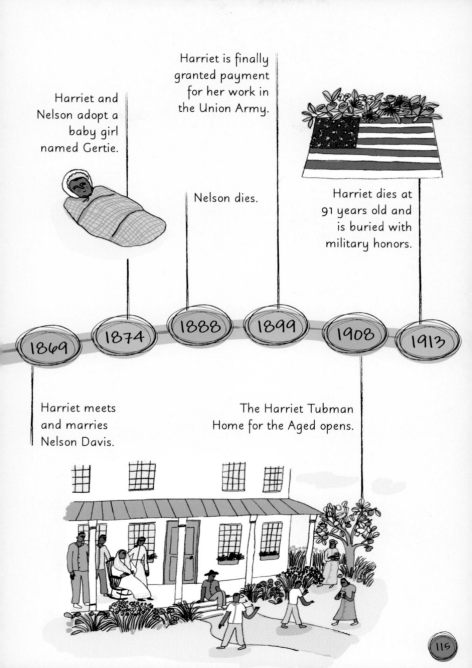

Harriet and Nelson adopt a baby girl named Gertie.

Harriet is finally granted payment for her work in the Union Army.

Nelson dies.

Harriet dies at 91 years old and is buried with military honors.

1869 1874 1888 1899 1908 1913

Harriet meets and marries Nelson Davis.

The Harriet Tubman Home for the Aged opens.

Quiz

 1. In which state was Harriet born?

 2. What food did Harriet get beaten for trying to take when she was young?

 3. Why did Harriet get hit on the head with a heavy weight?

 4. What did Harriet's deal with Brodess, in which she paid him $60 per year, allow her to do?

 5. What did Harriet give as a gift to the white woman who helped her get to a safe house?

 6. Who were the first enslaved people (besides herself) that Harriet helped to free?

 7. What was the name of the Canadian town that Harriet used as her base for her Underground Railroad rescue missions?

**Do you remember what you've read?
How many of these questions about
Harriet's life can you answer?**

 What nickname did Harriet get for helping so many enslaved people escape?

 Why didn't Harriet join John Brown on his raid on Harper's Ferry?

 What was the name of the Civil War raid that Harriet led, in which she helped free more than 700 enslaved people?

 How long did Harriet have to wait before she was paid for her work in the Union Army?

 Harriet was nominated to appear on what United States' currency?

Answers on page 128

Who's who?

54th Massachusetts Volunteer Infantry Regiment (1863–1865) regiment in the Union Army made up entirely of African American soldiers

Bradford, Sarah (1818–1912) abolitionist who wrote a biography of Harriet, *Scenes in the Life of Harriet Tubman*, in 1869

Brodess, Edward (1801–1849) white man who owned Harriet, her mother, and her siblings

Brodess, Eliza (c.1802–c.1858) Edward's wife, who inherited ownership of Harriet's family

Brown, John (1800–1859) well-known white abolitionist who led slave rebellions and believed violence was a necessary means to end slavery

Carney, William (1840–1908) sergeant in the 54th Massachusetts Regiment who was the first African American to win a Medal of Honor

Davis, Nelson (c.1840–1888) Civil War veteran; Harriet's second husband

Douglass, Frederick (1818–1895) celebrated author, human rights leader, and abolitionist who was born into slavery, secretly learned to read, and escaped north at age 20

Fillmore, Millard (1800–1874) 13th president of the United States, from 1850 to 1853

Garrett, Thomas (1789–1871) abolitionist who helped fund Harriet's rescue missions

Jackson, Jacob
(c.1800–1864) free African American farmer who could read and write; helped Harriet rescue her brothers

Lincoln, Abraham
(1809–1865) 16th president of the United States, from 1861 to 1865; issued the Emancipation Proclamation

Pattison, Atthow
(unknown–1797) Rit's original owner, who had agreed to free her at age 45

Queen Victoria
(1819–1901) queen of Great Britain from 1837 to 1901

Ross, Benjamin "Ben"
(c.1785–1871) Harriet's father

Ross, Harriet "Rit"
(c.1795–1880) Harriet's mother

Sanborn, Franklin B.
(1831–1917) journalist who publicized Harriet's role in the Combahee River Raid as well as her Underground Railroad rescue missions

Seward, William
(1801–1872) abolitionist, New York State governor, United States senator, and later, Secretary of State, from 1861 to 1869

Stewart, John
(1804–1889) farmer, merchant, and shipbuilder who employed Harriet and her father

Still, William
(1821–1902) free African American author and abolitionist

Thompson, Anthony
(c.1775–1836) plantation owner who owned Harriet's father; stepfather to Edward Brodess

Tubman, John
(1820–1867) free African American man; Harriet's first husband

Wilson, Hiram
(1803–1864) abolitionist and activist who set up schools for free black people; a prominent resident of St. Catharines, Canada, he helped Harriet prepare for her rescue missions south

Glossary

abolitionist
person who believed slavery should be abolished, or ended

arsenal
place where weapons and related equipment are stored and/or made

auction block
platform from which an auctioneer sells goods (including enslaved people)

auctioneer
person who runs an auction

boarders
people who live and have meals in someone else's home in exchange for pay

Civil War
war between the North (the Union) and the South (the Confederate States) from 1861 to 1865; the deadliest war on American soil

Confederate States
group of states that seceded (broke away) from the United States, which led to the Civil War

Constitution
document listing the basic laws of the United States and the rights of its citizens

contraband
term for fugitive slaves (slaves who escaped or were brought into Union territory) during the Civil War

corn crib
structure, usually built above ground, that is used to dry and store corn for animal feed

counter weight
heavy weight that was used to balance scales in stores

democracy
form of government in which citizens vote in order to help make decisions about how the country is run

Drinking Gourd / Big Dipper
constellation (group of stars in a shape) that looks like a ladle, or "dipper" to drink from, and was used by enslaved people to locate the North Star

emancipation
act of setting someone free from control or slavery

Emancipation Proclamation
law that freed all the slaves; went into effect from 1863

execution
act of killing someone as a legal penalty

flax
plant whose fibers are used to make rope or coarse fabric

Fugitive Slave Act
law that made it legal to capture and return enslaved people who had run away from their owners, even if they were living in a free state

hallucinations
dreamlike states in which someone sees or hears things that are not really there

jubilee
season of celebration; how enslaved people referred to emancipation for all

manumission
when someone is released from slavery

muskrats
short-legged rodents, about the size of two rats, that live in marshes, swamps, and wetlands of North America

North Star
bright star in the Drinking Gourd / Big Dipper constellation; used by enslaved people to navigate north

overseer
manager who is responsible for enslaved people's work and crop production on a large farm

peninsula
piece of land jutting into the water

perilous
dangerous

plantation
huge farm where crops were grown and harvested, which depended on enslaved Africans to do the work

plight
difficult situation

regiment
unit of an army

secede
separate from an organization, such as a country

seizure
sudden attack during which a person experiences convulsions and may become unconscious

slave auction
sale of enslaved men, women, and children to the highest bidder

slavecatcher
person who captured runaway slaves and returned them to their owners for money

slavery
when a person is controlled and "owned" by another

stationmaster
person who was part of the Underground Railroad and helped enslaved people escape

Underground Railroad
network of safe routes
and places, started by
abolitionists who secretly
offered guidance and care
for runaway slaves on their
way north to freedom

Union
Northern states that did
not become part of the
Confederate States during
the Civil War

vision
something dreamed or
imagined, especially as
part of a religious or
supernatural experience

wharf
structure built along a body
of water that enables boats
to load or unload passengers
and cargo

women's suffrage
women's right to vote,
which was not gained in
the United States until 1920

Index

13th Amendment 91

54th Massachusetts Volunteer Infantry Regiment 89–90

Aa

abolition / abolitionists 12, 27, 49, 55, 60–61, 64, 65, 71, 73–75, 78, 86, 93, 102

African Americans 14, 21, 24, 48, 50, 64, 73, 81, 83, 86, 90, 91, 98

Alfred (Kizzy's son) 54

Araminta (Kizzy's daughter) 54

Auburn, New York 74–76, 92, 104, 106

auction block 30, 36, 44

Bb

Baltimore 55

Big Dipper 42, 57

birth, Harriet's 30

birthdays, slave 30

boarders 94–95

Bradford, Sarah 94

Brodess, Edward 16, 17, 18, 19, 20, 24, 27, 28, 30, 33–35, 36, 37, 38

Brodess, Eliza 17, 37, 38, 40, 52, 68

Brown, John 73–74, 76–79

Cc

Canada 13, 57, 61–65, 73

Carney, William 90

Chesapeake Bay 16, 55, 86

childhood, Harriet's 16–22

churches 72

civil rights 103

Civil War 82–91, 93, 102

codes, secret 56–58, 86

Combahee River Raid 88, 89

conductors 14, 56, 57, 61

Confederate Army 82, 83, 87, 89, 91

Confederate States 82, 84–85, 87

Congress 82

contraband 86

corn cribs 67, 68

Dd

Davis, Gertie (adopted daughter) 94, 97

Davis, Nelson (2nd husband) 94, 97

124

death, Harriet's 120
Deep South 37
Douglass, Frederick 60–61, 94

Ee
elderly, work for the 92, 99
emancipation 27, 78
Emancipation Proclamation 87, 88

Ff
Fillmore, Millard 51
flax 24–25
Fort Sumpter, South Carolina 82, 83
free men / women 28, 29, 32–33, 46–47, 58
free states 10, 11, 29, 47, 50, 51
Fugitive Slave Act 51, 56, 61, 74
fugitive slaves 8, 51, 52, 64, 69, 75, 86

Gg
Garrett, Thomas 71
Glory (film) 90
goodbye song, Harriet's 44
grave, Harriet's 100, 106–107

Hh
hallucinations 26
Harper's Ferry, West Virginia 76, 78
Harriet Tubman Home for the Aged 99
head injury 26, 100

Ii
ill health 20, 26, 36, 78, 91, 92, 100
income 34–35, 92, 93, 94, 95, 103

Jj
Jackson, Jacob 33
James (Kizzy's son) 54
Jamestown, Virginia 10

Kk
Keziah (Kizzy) (cousin) 37, 38, 40, 52, 54, 55, 72
kidnappers 50

Ll
Lake Ontario 61
legacy, Harriet's 102–108
Lincoln, Abraham 75, 81, 82, 86, 87, 91

Mm

manumission 27, 28
marriage, Harriet's 32–33
Mary Anne *see* Keziah
     (Kizzy)
Maryland 9, 13, 16, 38, 49,
     52, 54, 58, 66, 73, 78
military service 88–90, 93
monuments and memorials
     103–105
muskrats 20

Nn

names, Harriet's 8, 13, 48,
     71, 74, 77, 104, 108
Niagara Falls Suspension
     Bridge 61, 62–63, 64,
     70, 72, 80
North Star 9, 42, 43, 57
nursing 14, 86, 93

Oo

overseers 25

Pp

passengers 57, 65
Pattison, Atthow 38
Philadelphia 13, 46, 48–50,
     52, 58, 70
plantations 35
punishments 22, 26, 45

Rr

racism 93
reading 21, 33, 58, 93, 107
refugees 72
rescue missions 14, 58–60,
     65, 66–71, 72, 80–81,
     102, 107
revolts, slave 21, 73, 76–78
rewards 42
rights 41, 64, 98, 103
Rochester, New York 60,
     70
Ross, Ben (brother) 40, 41,
     42, 44, 67, 69, 72
Ross, Ben (father) 16, 17
     18, 27–28, 68, 69–70,
     72, 73, 75–76, 92
Ross, Henry (brother)
     40, 41, 42, 44, 59–60
Ross, Linah (sister) 40
Ross, Mariah Ritty (sister) 18
Ross, Rit (mother) 16, 18,
     20, 22, 28, 38, 44,
     68–70, 72, 73, 75–76,
     92, 94
Ross, Robert (brother) 67,
     69, 72

Ss

safe houses 45, 55, 57, 58,
     70, 71
sailors 29

sale of enslaved people 9,
      18, 27, 30, 35, 36, 37,
      38, 40
Sanborn, Franklin B. 87
Seward, William 75, 94
slave auctions 30, 36, 38
slavecatchers 46, 55, 56,
      67, 68
slave owners 9, 27, 28, 33,
      46, 50, 51, 89
slave revolts 21, 73, 76–78
slavery 8–14, 24, 27,
      30, 35, 50, 73–74,
      80–83, 86
spy, Harriet as 14, 88, 102
stars, navigating by 9, 29,
      42, 43
stationmasters 41, 45, 57,
      58
St. Catharines (Canada)
      61, 64–65, 66, 69
Stewart, John 28
Still, William 71
suffrage 98, 102

Tt

Thompson, Anthony 16,
      17, 27, 69
Trans-Atlantic Slave Trade
      10
Tubman, John (1st husband)
      32–33, 37, 41, 59

Uu

Underground Railroad
      11–13, 14, 41, 50, 56–65,
      66–71, 72, 75, 80–81,
      89, 102
Union Army 82, 83, 87, 88,
      95
Union States 82, 84–85, 86
United States, slavery in 10,
      21, 64, 74, 80–82

Vv

visions, Harriet's 27, 52
voting 72, 98

Ww

Washington, D.C. 91
wharves 29, 41
widow's pension 95
Wilson, Reverend Hiram
      65
women's rights 98, 102
writing 33, 93

Acknowledgments

The author would like to thank: Harriet herself for being an example to us all; Rosemary Sadlier for consulting and sharing information about Harriet; Charlotte Ager for her adorable illustrations; Shannon Beatty for her thoughtful edits; and everyone else who worked on this book.

DK would like to thank: Jacqueline Hornberger for proofreading; Becky Herrick for the resource section; Helen Peters for the index; Seeta Parmar for additional editorial help; Kanika Kalra for additional design help; Emily Kimball and Annie Lachmansingh for legal advice; Rosemary Sadlier for her expertise on Harriet's life and work; Angela Crenshaw and the Harriet Tubman Underground Railroad State Park for helpful input; Stephanie Laird for literacy consulting; and Noah Harley for serving as our "Kid Editor."

The publisher would like to thank the following for their kind permission to reproduce their photographs:
(Key: a-above; b-below/bottom; c-center; f-far; l-left; r-right; t-top)
15 Alamy Stock Photo: World History Archive.
20 Dreamstime.com: Paul Reeves (bl). 21 Alamy Stock Photo: North Wind Picture Archives (b). 24 Dreamstime.com: Sergey Kolesnikov (bl). 26 Dreamstime.com: Stefan Rotter (tr). 35 Getty Images: Bettmann (b). 36 Getty Images: DeAgostini (b). 46 Alamy Stock Photo: North Wind Picture Archives (c). 49 Getty Images: HultonArchive / Illustrated London News (t). 51 Getty Images: Bettmann (cra). 53 Library of Congress, Washington, D.C.: Emily Howland photograph album / LC-DIG-ppmsca-54230. 55 Getty Images: Archive Photos (t). 60 Getty Images: George Rinhart / Corbis (br). 62–63 Alamy Stock Photo: National Geographic Image Collection. 64 Alamy Stock Photo: Old Paper Studios (b). 67 Alamy Stock Photo: Dasan Dznananovic Daci (crb). 71 Rex by Shutterstock: F A Archive (tr). 73 Alamy Stock Photo: North Wind Picture Archives (crb). 75 Alamy Stock Photo: North Wind Picture Archives (tr). Getty Images: Epics (b). 79 Alamy Stock Photo: Painting. 81 Alamy Stock Photo: Stocktrek Images, Inc. (br). 83 Alamy Stock Photo: Harry Lands (b). Bridgeman Images:

American School, (19th century) / Confederate Memorial Hall, New Orleans, Louisiana, USA / Photo © Civil War Archive (c/Escort flag); Forbes, Mrs. John E. (fl.1861-63) / Collection of the New-York Historical Society, USA (c). 87 Alamy Stock Photo: Pictorial Press Ltd (c). 90 Getty Images: TriStar Pictures / Sunset Boulevard / Corbis (c). 96–97 Getty Images: MPI. 98 Alamy Stock Photo: Still Light (cra). 101 Getty Images: The Print Collector. 103 Alamy Stock Photo: Anthony Pleva (br). 104 Getty Images: Bettmann (bl). 105 Alamy Stock Photo: Jim West. 106 National Museum of African American History and Culture: Collection of the Smithsonian National Museum of (tl). 109 Alamy Stock Photo: North Wind Picture Archives. 111 Library of Congress, Washington, D.C.: Emily Howland photograph album / LC-DIG-ppmsca-54230 (bl)

Cover images: Front: Library of Congress, Washington, D.C.: Emily Howland photograph album / LC-DIG-ppmsca-54230; Spine: Library of Congress, Washington, D.C.: Emily Howland photograph album / LC-DIG-ppmsca-54230 ca

All other images © Dorling Kindersley
For further information see: www.dkimages.com

ANSWERS TO THE QUIZ ON PAGES 116–117

1. Maryland; 2. a sugar cube; 3. she was trying to protect another enslaved person from his overseer; 4. work for herself, and keep any money she earned over $60; 5. a quilt she'd made from scraps; 6. her niece Kizzy and Kizzy's family; 7. St. Catharines; 8. Moses; 9. she was sick; 10. the Combahee River Raid; 11. 35 years; 12. the $20 bill